P9-CEY-671

PORTRAITS OF THE STATES

by Mary Dykstra

**Please visit our web site at: www.garethstevens.com**
**For a free color catalog describing Gareth Stevens Publishing's list of high-quality books, call 1-800-542-2595 (USA) or 1-800-387-3178 (Canada).**

**Library of Congress Cataloging-in-Publication Data**

Dykstra, Mary, 1952-
Iowa / Mary Dykstra.
p. cm. — (Portraits of the states)
Includes bibliographical references and index.
ISBN-13: 978-0-8368-4664-5 (lib. bdg.)
ISBN-10: 0-8368-4664-8 (lib. bdg.)
ISBN-13: 978-0-8368-4683-6 (softcover)
ISBN-10: 0-8368-4683-4 (softcover)
1. Iowa—Juvenile literature. I. Title. II. Series.
F621.3.D95 2006
977.7—dc22 2005044475

This North American edition first published in 2006 by
**Gareth Stevens Publishing**
A Weekly Reader® Company
1 Reader's Digest Road
Pleasantville, NY 10570-7000 USA



Editorial direction: Mark J. Sachner
Project manager: Jonatha A. Brown
Editor: Catherine Gardner
Art direction and design: Tammy West
Picture research: Diane Laska-Swanke
Indexer: Walter Kronenberg
Production: Jessica Morris and Robert Kraus

Picture credits: Cover, © Don Eastman; p. 4 © James P. Rowan; p. 5 © Corel; pp. 6, 7, 27 © Library of Congress; pp. 9, 11, 18, 21, 26, 29 Iowa Tourism Office; p. 12 © Frances Miller/Time & Life Pictures/Getty Images; p. 15 © ArtToday; pp. 16, 22 © PhotoDisc; pp. 24, 25 © Gibson Stock Photography; p. 28 © Elsa/ Getty Images



Printed in the United States of America

3 4 5 6 7 8 9 11 10 09 08 07

# CONTENTS



Words that are defined in the Glossary appear in **bold** the first time they are used in the text.

On the Cover: The capitol in Des Moines is the home of Iowa's state government.

# Introduction

When you think of Iowa, do you think of long rows of corn? Many people do. Iowa is well known for its cornfields. Yet, the state has much more to offer. It has big cities and fun festivals.

Iowa is like a crossroads. Here, country life meets city life. Farms and factories work together. They produce food for people all over the world.

The past and present meet in Iowa, too. Years ago, settlers came to Iowa from Europe. Some people who live in Iowa now can trace their families back to those times. Modern museums in Iowa teach about the past.

Iowans want to show you their state. Come for a visit!

**Iowa produces more corn than any other state in the nation.**

The state flag of Iowa.

# IOWA FACTS

- Became the 29th U.S. State: December 28, 1846
- Population (2005): 2,966,334
- Capital: Des Moines
- Biggest Cities: Des Moines, Cedar Rapids, Davenport, Sioux City
- Size: 55,869 square miles (144,701 square kilometers)
- Nickname: The Hawkeye State
- State Tree: Oak
- State Flower: Wild rose
- State Bird: Eastern goldfinch
- State Song: "The Song of Iowa"

# History

The first people to live in Iowa were Native Americans. They came to the area thousands of years ago. The Native peoples hunted animals, grew crops, and made clay pots. They built huge mounds of dirt. The mounds were a place to bury people after they died.

## The French Come to Iowa

Louis Jolliet and Jacques Marquette were the first Europeans to see Iowa. They were French explorers. In 1673, the two men paddled canoes a long way. They reached the Mississippi River. Then, they came to the area that is now Iowa.

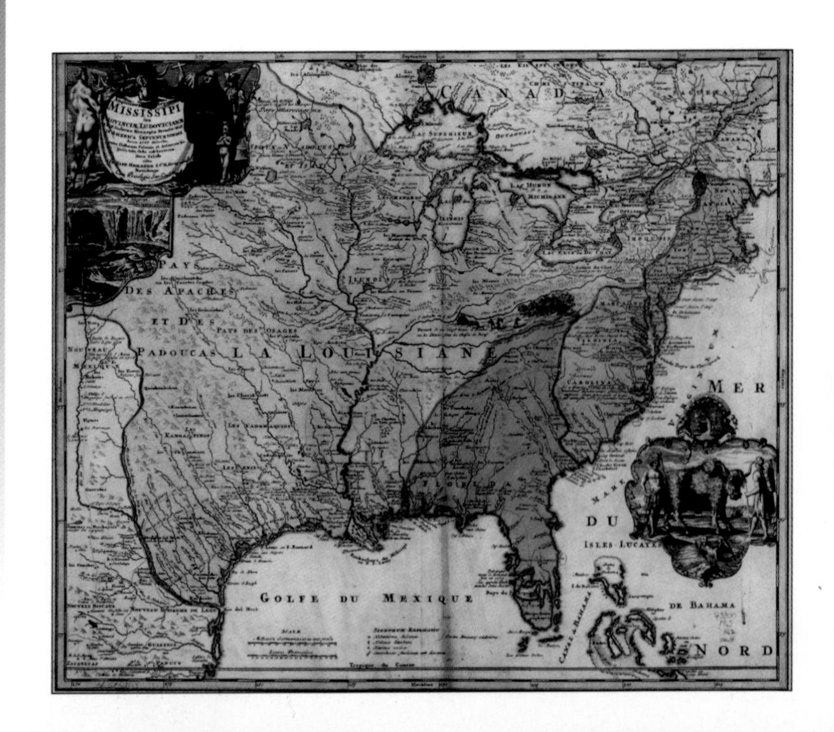


This old map is from 1763. The land in yellow was held by France. In the middle of the map, the Mississippi River runs past what is now Iowa.

**Iowa's Name**

The name *Iowa* may have more than one meaning. Some people think the name came from a Native word for "beautiful land." Others think it came from a word that means "one who puts to sleep."

## France Sells the Land

By 1682, Iowa was part of a large piece of land owned by France. The French named the land Louisiana after their king, Louis. The United States bought the land in 1803. The deal was known as the Louisiana Purchase.

Other French people soon followed the first explorers. They found animals to hunt and trap for fur. They also found **lead**. Nicolas Perrot taught Native people how to **mine** lead. He also traded with the Native people.

Later, Julien Dubuque became the state's first white settler. He was a lead miner. A city near the place where he lived now bears his name. Some trappers and hunters moved to the area, too.

**In the 1800s, many settlers came to Iowa to buy cheap land for farming.**

**Iowa Decides**

Since 1846, Iowans have played a big part in choosing the people who run for U.S. president. In an election year, Iowans gather in groups called caucuses. They choose the person they will support. The Iowa Caucuses are held very early in the election year. Newspapers and TV stations give a lot of attention to these Caucuses.

## Lewis and Clark

The United States now owned a big new **territory**. In 1804, President Thomas Jefferson sent Meriwether Lewis and William Clark to explore the land. The two men and their crew started their trip in boats. They mapped the land as they traveled through it.

The journey took Lewis and Clark along the Missouri River in western Iowa. One of their crew died while they were there. His grave is near Sioux City.

**Famous People of Iowa**

### Amelia Jenks Bloomer

**Born:** May 27, 1818, Homer, New York

**Died:** December 30, 1894, Council Bluffs, Iowa

Amelia Jenks Bloomer started *The Lily* newspaper in 1849. It was one of the first newspapers in the nation written by and for women. She wanted women to have the right to vote. She made many speeches about women's rights. Bloomer wore a skirt over baggy pants. The outfit was named the "bloomer" after her. Soon, other women wore bloomers, too. Bloomers stood for women's rights.

**First Female Lawyer**

Arabella Babb Mansfield was the first woman in the United States to become a lawyer. She was born on a farm in Des Moines County. She became a lawyer in 1869. At the time, she was only twenty-three years old. She proved that women could do a job that only men had done in the past.

## Soldiers and Settlers

Zebulon Pike explored the eastern part of the state. He looked for good places to build forts. In 1808, Fort Madison was founded on the Mississippi River. The fort housed U.S. soldiers.

In the early 1800s, most people who moved to Iowa were Native Americans. Settlers and soldiers had pushed them off the land to the east. The Black Hawk War broke out in 1832 because the Native people tried to go back to their homes. They lost the war and had to move farther west. White settlers moved into the eastern part of Iowa.

**The Hitchcock House is in Lewis. In the 1800s, it was a stop on Iowa's Underground Railroad.**

## A U.S. State

In 1838, the United States formed the Iowa Territory. All of Iowa and parts of some other states were in the territory. Iowa became a U.S. state in 1846.

Settlers soon streamed into the new state. Many were from New York and Ohio. Most people came to Iowa because the land was good for farming. As more settlers arrived, they pushed Native people farther west.

## Civil War

In the mid-1800s, the United States was divided. Many people in the South wanted to own slaves. In the North, most people thought it was wrong to own slaves. Iowa was part of the North. In 1861, Southern states formed their own nation. The nation was called the Confederate States of America.

The North and South started to fight the Civil War. Men from Iowa fought for the North. They went to other states to fight battles.

The Civil War went on for four years. After the war ended in 1865, Iowa let black children go to public school. African Americans gained the right to vote.

### IN IOWA'S HISTORY

**Underground Railroad**

In the time of the Civil War, some people in Iowa helped slaves escape. The slaves ran away from the South. The Iowans hid the slaves in their houses and barns. The slaves rested and ate. Then, they kept moving north. The slaves moved in secret from house to house. The people who helped were part of a network called the Underground Railroad.

Covered bridges like this one were built in Iowa many years ago.

## New Ways to Travel

Steamboats started to carry goods on the Mississippi River in the 1800s. The steamboats changed the way people lived in Iowa. Cities along the river grew.

Railroads changed Iowa, too. Four railroads crossed the state by 1870. They made some small towns rich. People in the towns could use trains to transport goods for sale. From 1870 to 1920, Iowa's farms fed much of the nation.

## Hard Times

Many farmers lost their land during the **Great Depression** in the 1930s. This was a time when crop prices fell. The farmers had borrowed money from banks to pay for their land. When the farmers could not make their payments, the banks took the farmers' land.

The United States fought in World War II during the 1940s. The nation needed pork and corn products to

### IN IOWA'S HISTORY

**Covered Bridges**

In the late 1800s, many covered bridges were built in Iowa. The bridges were covered to protect their floors. It cost more to make a new floor than to cover the sides and roof of the bridge. Madison County still has five of these bridges. Today, people come to see Iowa's famous covered bridges.

**Farming has played a big part in Iowa's history. The state's farmers have fed Americans during war and peace.**

help feed the people who were fighting in the war. This new demand helped the farmers in Iowa.

**Move from the Farms**

After World War II, many factories were built in Iowa cities. The factories offered jobs to the people in Iowa. People moved to cities as **industries** there grew. By the 1960s, more Iowans lived in cities than in the country.

In the 1980s, the state went through hard times again. Crop prices fell. Many farmers had to stop farming. People left the state to look for work in other places.

After a few years, prices for crops rose again. Iowa still has many farms today. Some of these farms are much larger than the farms people had long ago.

**IN IOWA'S HISTORY**

**Early Computers**

An Iowa teacher and his student helped change the world. In 1939, John V. Atanasoff and Clifford Berry invented a new type of computer. They built the computer at Iowa State University. Other scientists later used their design to make the earliest types of computers.

# Time Line

| | |
|---|---|
| **1673** | Louis Jolliet and Father Jacques Marquette explore the Mississippi River. |
| **1788** | Julien Dubuque becomes the first white person to settle in Iowa. |
| **1803** | The Louisiana Purchase brings Iowa into the United States. |
| **1808** | The U.S. Army sets up a military post in Fort Madison. |
| **1832** | The U.S. Army defeats Native Americans in the Black Hawk War. |
| **1838** | The United States forms the Iowa Territory. |
| **1846** | Iowa becomes the twenty-ninth U.S. state. |
| **1857** | Des Moines becomes the state capital. |
| **1868** | Iowa gives African American men the right to vote. |
| **1884** | The capitol building is completed in Des Moines. |
| **1928** | Iowa-born Herbert Hoover is elected president of the United States. |
| **1941** | The United States enters World War II. The new need for farm products helps Iowa farmers. |
| **1960** | For the first time, more Iowans live in cities than in rural areas. |
| **1993** | Floods damage land across the state. |

# People

Some Native peoples lived in Iowa for thousands of years. Others moved there when white people took their lands in other parts of the country. The Natives tried to win back their land. They lost it in the Black Hawk War.

## White Settlers

After 1832, Native people began to lose their land in Iowa, too. The land was sold to white settlers who wanted to buy it.

**Hispanics:** In the 2000 U.S. Census, 2.8 percent of the people in Iowa called themselves Latino or Hispanic. Most of them or their relatives came from places where Spanish is spoken. They may come from different racial backgrounds.

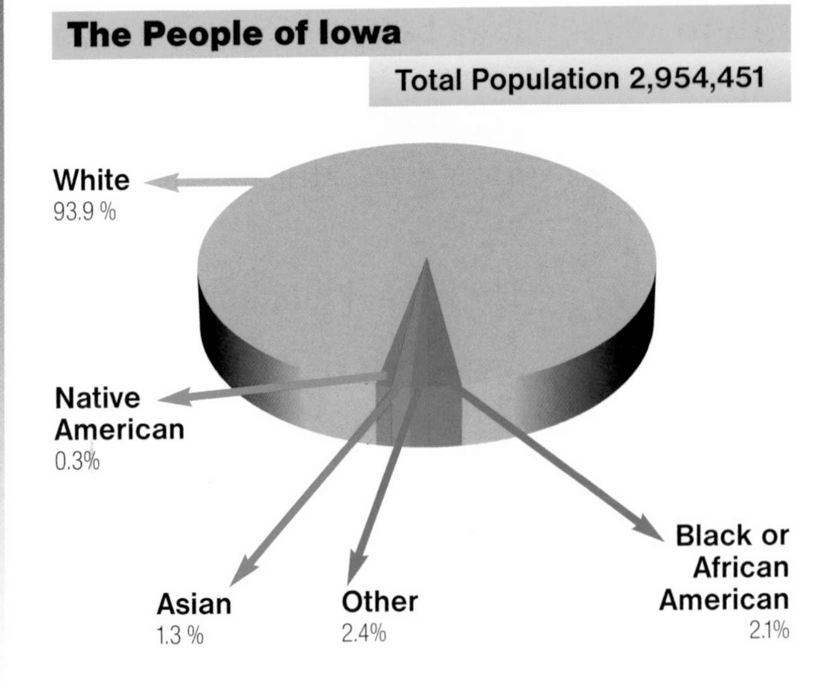


Percentages are based on the 2000 Census.

These settlers came to Iowa in a covered wagon. Their wagon probably held everything they owned.

Settlers from the East soon streamed into Iowa. At first, they used covered wagons. Later, people went west by train.

People also came from Europe. They crossed the sea by ship. Some people were from Germany and Norway. Others came from Ireland and England.

When they reached the United States, some of the **immigrants** went to Iowa. Most of these people became farmers. Together, they founded small towns and villages. Some places in Iowa still keep alive the old customs from Europe. They cook German or Swedish foods. They play music and dance the way their **ancestors** did.

### Iowa People Today

In recent years, people have moved to Iowa from Mexico and other places where Spanish is spoken. Other people have come from Asia. Now, people from all around the world live in Iowa. Even

Des Moines, Iowa's capital as well as its largest city, sits on the Des Moines River.

so, eight out of ten people who live in Iowa were born in the state.

About 2 percent of the people in the state are African American. This number is much lower than in most states.

Iowa is home to almost three million people. For a long time, more people lived in rural areas than in cities. Iowa still has many farmers. Today, however, more people live in cities and towns than on farms. The biggest cities in the state are Des Moines, Cedar Rapids, Davenport, and Sioux City.

### Education

In 1830, a doctor started the first public school near Keokuk. Nine years later, the whole state had public schools. Today, Iowa has the highest **literacy** rate in the United States.

The state's first public library opened in 1853. In the early 1930s, the David W. Smouse Opportunity School opened its doors in Des Moines. It was one of the first public schools in the country for children with disabilities.

The state has many fine colleges. The oldest one is the University of Iowa in Iowa City. It is famous for its Writers' Workshop. Its students learn writing skills from well-known authors and poets.

Ames is home to Iowa State University. The state's private colleges include Drake and Grinnell.

## Famous People of Iowa

### Black Hawk

**Born:** 1767, near Rock Island, Illinois

**Died:** October 1838, near the Des Moines River, Iowa

Black Hawk was a chief and warrior of the Sauk people. The Sauk lived in what is now Illinois. They were forced to move to Iowa. In 1832, Black Hawk led the Sauk and Fox people in a war to get back their land. They lost the war. Black Hawk and his people had to stay in Iowa. The war was named after Black Hawk. Iowa's nickname, Hawkeye State, probably comes from Black Hawk's name.

### Religion

Nine out of ten people in Iowa are Christians. Most of the Christians belong to Protestant churches. Other Christians are Catholic. A small number of people in the state are Jewish. Many Muslims make their homes in Cedar Rapids.

# The Land

Huge sheets of ice covered most of Iowa before people lived there. The weight of these **glaciers** flattened the land. Over a period of many years, all of the ice melted. The glaciers left behind a thick layer of rich soil. Iowa has more of this rich soil than any other state.

Years of farming have caused damage to the land. Some of the soil has blown or washed away. The top layer of soil is now much thinner.

The land in Iowa, however, is still very good for growing crops. Farmers now plow and plant their fields in ways that prevent **erosion**.

## High Spots

Some people think all of Iowa is flat, but that is not true. The northeastern part was not flattened by glaciers. There, tall

**Parts of northwestern and northeastern Iowa are hilly.**

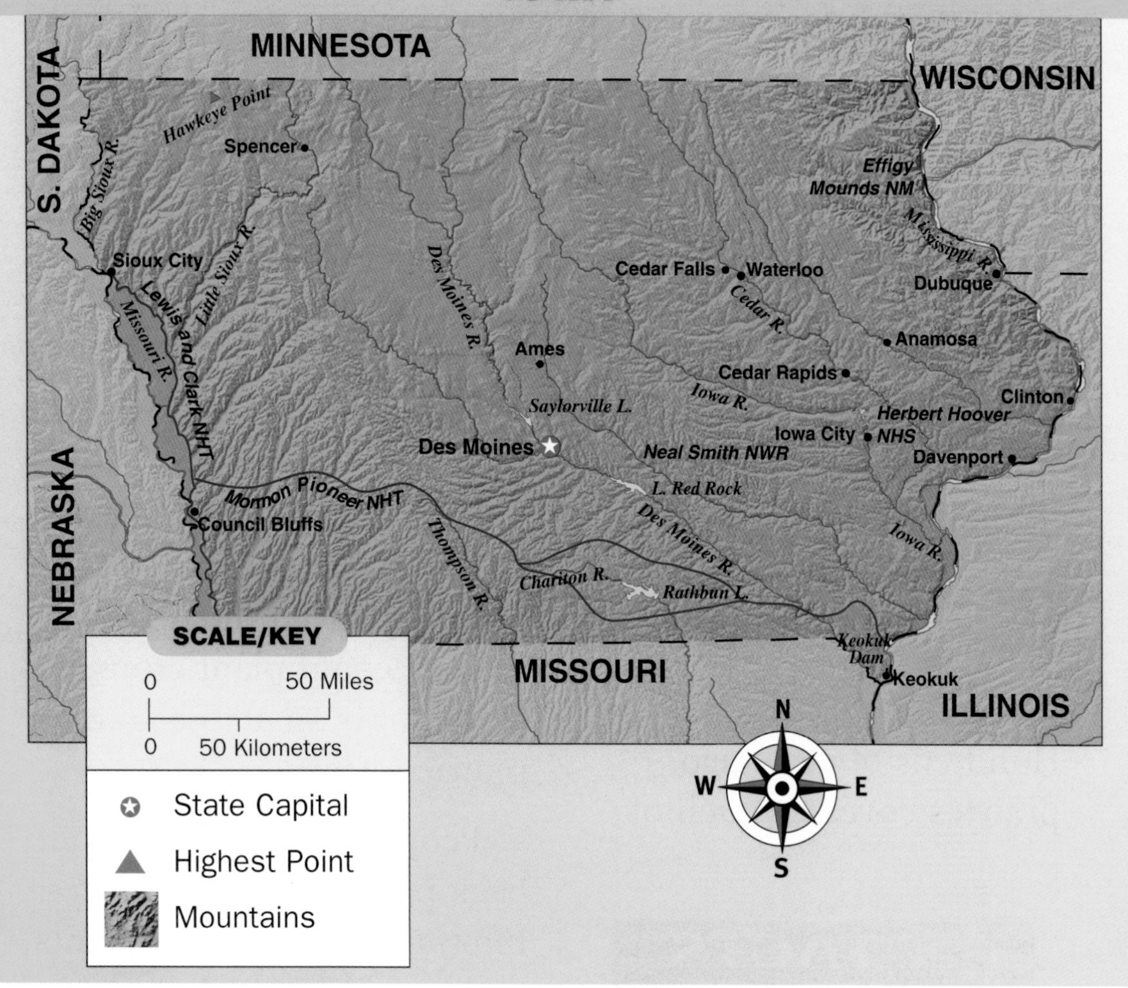


**bluffs** line the Mississippi River.

At Pikes Peak State Park, trails run along the bluff. Hikers can see boats on the water below. Many people come to this part of the state in the fall to see the colorful trees.

Hawkeye Point is the highest point in the state. It is 1,670 feet (509 meters) high. Hawkeye Point is in the northwestern corner of the state.

## Lakes and Rivers

Rivers run along both sides of Iowa. The Mississippi

River forms the border on the eastern side of the state. The Missouri River forms most of the state's western border. The Big Sioux River completes the border on the western side.

Small rivers flow through Iowa, too. The state also has many lakes and ponds. These waterways make good **habitats** for wildlife.

### Saving the Prairies

Hundreds of years ago, **prairies** covered much of Iowa. Herds of buffalo lived on the prairies. Then, the settlers plowed the prairies so they could plant crops. Today, only small pieces of prairie remain.

People are working to put back prairies in some places. First, they remove the plants that would not be found on a prairie. Then, they plant seeds of grass and flowers that lived there long ago.

### Wildlife on the Land

Early settlers also cut down many trees. The forests that are left are home to many animals. Deer and squirrels

**Major Rivers**

**Missouri River**
2,466 miles (3,968 km) long

**Mississippi River**
2,357 miles (3,792 km) long

**Des Moines River**
535 miles (861 km) long

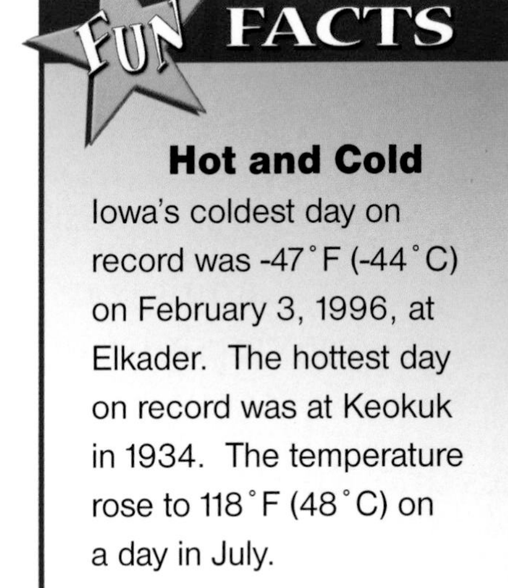


**Hot and Cold**

Iowa's coldest day on record was -47°F (-44°C) on February 3, 1996, at Elkader. The hottest day on record was at Keokuk in 1934. The temperature rose to 118°F (48°C) on a day in July.

**Crystal Rocks**

Iowa's state rock is the geode. Geodes have a hard outside shell, but they are hollow on the inside. Sparkling crystals line the inside of a geode.

live in Iowa's forests. Foxes and other animals can also be found there.

Northwest Iowa has large areas of flat, open plains. Jackrabbits live on these plains. Gophers and snakes are found there, too.

## Birds and Fish

Many types of birds live in Iowa all year round. Bald eagles hunt for fish along rivers. Cardinals and blue jays also live in the state all during the year.

The eastern goldfinch is the state bird. It can be seen at any time of year. Flocks of finches visit bird feeders in winter.

Other birds come to Iowa only for part of the year. Ducks and geese fly through the state in spring and fall. Bluebirds and orioles are colorful birds. They can be seen most often during spring and summer.

The streams of northeast Iowa are home to bass and trout. Bluegills, walleye, and catfish swim in the state's lakes and rivers.

**The Mississippi River runs along the eastern border of Iowa. Many towns and cities have grown up on the banks of the river.**

# Economy

Iowa is well known for its farms. It is sometimes called the Corn State. More corn comes from Iowa than from any other state.

## Other Farm Products

Soybeans, oats, and hay are other crops grown in the state. About 90 percent of the land in Iowa is farmland.

Iowa leads the nation in hog farming. Iowa farmers raise one-fourth of the hogs in the United States. Many of the state's farmers also raise cattle.

Iowa's farms don't just make jobs for farmers. They create jobs in cities, too.

Barges carry heavy loads up and down the Mississippi River.

Factory workers turn farm crops into food products. They make corn oil and cereal. The factories in Iowa also make a lot of farm equipment.

## Other Jobs

Insurance is big business in Iowa. Many of the state's insurance companies are in Des Moines. Publishing has grown in Iowa during recent years. Publishing companies in Des Moines make many magazines and books.

Many people have service jobs. These jobs help other people. Teachers, doctors, and hotel workers are some kinds of service workers.

Tourism creates lots of service jobs. Each year, many tourists come to Iowa. They visit museums, parks, and other sites in the state. All of these places need service workers.

### How Money Is Made in Iowa

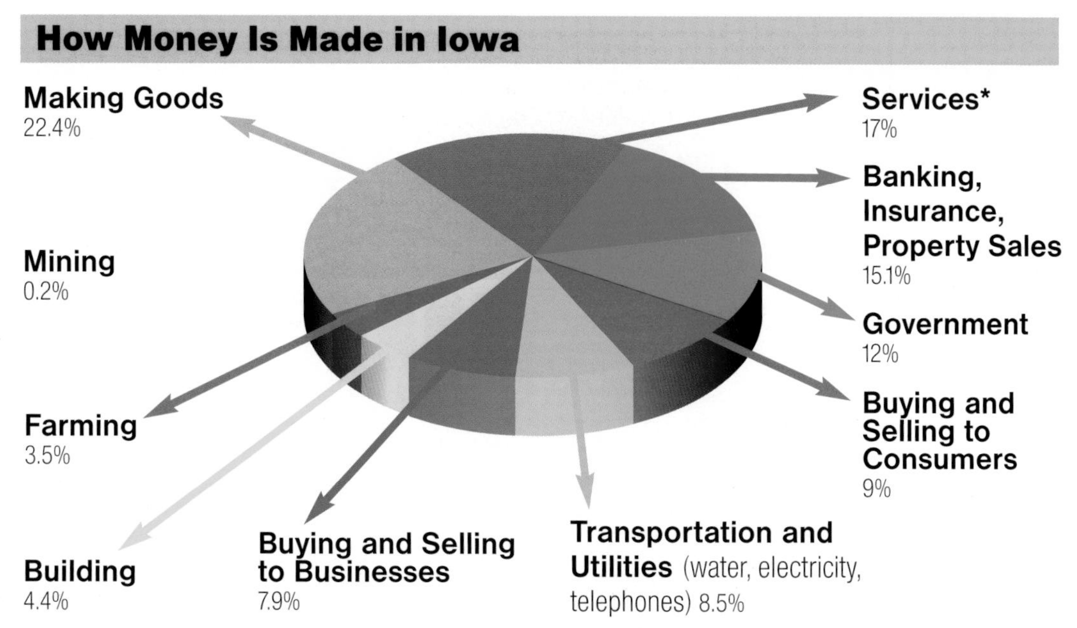


* Services include jobs in hotels, restaurants, auto repair, medicine, teaching, and entertainment.

# Government

Des Moines is the capital of Iowa. The leaders of the state work there. The state government has three parts, called branches. The parts are the executive, legislative, and judicial branches.

### Executive Branch

The executive branch carries out the state's laws. The governor is the head of this branch. The lieutenant governor helps the governor.

### Legislative Branch

The legislative branch makes laws for the state. The Iowa **legislature** is called

The state capitol in Des Moines has a beautiful dome covered with thin sheets of gold.

The Governor's Mansion stands tall in Iowa's capital city.

## Judicial Branch

Judges and courts make up the judicial branch. Judges and courts may decide whether people who have been accused of committing crimes are guilty.

## Local Governments

The state of Iowa is made up of ninety-nine counties. Most counties are run by a group of three people who are elected. Cities have a mayor and city council to lead them.

the General Assembly. It has two parts, the Senate and the House of Representatives. The two parts work together to make laws.

## IOWA'S STATE GOVERNMENT

**Executive**

| Office | Length of Term |
|---|---|
| Governor | 4 years |
| Lieutenant Governor | 4 Years |

**Legislative**

| Body | Length of Term |
|---|---|
| Senate (50 members) | 4 years |
| House of Representatives (100 members) | 2 years |

**Judicial**

| Court | Length of Term |
|---|---|
| Supreme (7 justices) | 8 years |
| Appeals (9judges) | 6 years |

# Things to See and Do

FUN FACTS

**College Sports**

Iowans love to watch their college teams play sports. Football is big at the University of Iowa. Its team, the Hawkeyes, has many fans. Drake University is known for track and field. Drake hosts a major track meet every year. Basketball, hockey, and other sports are also popular in Iowa.

Iowa is full of history and fun. At **Effigy Mounds** National Monument, visitors learn about the early peoples of Iowa. This park has almost two hundred mounds. Hiking trails go past the mounds. Some of these mounds are in the shapes of animals. The biggest group has ten bear shapes and three bird shapes.

West Branch is home to the Herbert Hoover National Historic Site. Its museum teaches about President Herbert Hoover.

**People who like baseball visit a playing field in Dyersville. This field was used in the movie *Field of Dreams*. The movie told a story about players from long ago.**

## River World

The National Mississippi River Museum and Aquarium is in Dubuque. It has five big aquariums. It has many other things to see, too. People who visit can look at boats and learn all about them. A trail leads hikers to places where they can watch herons, frogs, and other wildlife.

On the Fourth of July, boaters go to Clinton for Riverboat Days. The event is fun for people of all ages. Shoppers look for bargains in the flea market. Kids enjoy the circus and petting zoo.

In Davenport, music lovers can tap their toes to good music. A museum there celebrates the music that was created along the Mississippi River. The River Music

### Famous People of Iowa

## Herbert Hoover

**Born:** August 10, 1874, West Branch, Iowa

**Died:** October 20, 1964, New York City, New York

Herbert Hoover was born in West Branch. His parents died when he was nine years old. Hoover went to live with his uncle. When he grew up, Hoover worked in mining. Then he worked to help poor people in Europe who needed food. In 1929, Hoover became the thirty-first U.S. president. The Great Depression started while Hoover was president. Some people blamed him for those hard times. Hoover is the only U.S. president who was born in Iowa.

**Sharp Turns Ahead!**
Snake Alley is known as "the crookedest street in the world." It packs seven sharp turns into one short, steep stretch of road in the city of Burlington.

Experience has theaters and displays.

People who visit can learn about jazz, rock 'n' roll, and the blues. Children have an area where they can make their own music.

## Sports and Outdoors

Iowa has more than eighty state parks. Some of these parks are on historic sites. Maquoketa Caves State Park has caves of all sizes and shapes. People who visit have to crawl to get through some of the caves.

Big crowds turn out to watch college basketball games in Iowa. Here, the Iowa Hawkeyes drive down the court in a game against the Cincinnati Bearcats.

Each year, Onawa hosts a Lewis & Clark Festival. Visitors can ride on a boat like one used by Lewis and Clark long ago.

## Famous People of Iowa

### Grant Wood

**Born:** February 13, 1892, Anamosa, Iowa

**Died:** February 12, 1942, Iowa City, Iowa

Grant Wood was a famous painter. Many of his paintings were of people and places in Iowa. Some showed the state's rolling hills and farms. His best-known painting is *American Gothic*. It shows a farmer and his daughter in front of their house. Many of his paintings are displayed at the Cedar Rapids Museum of Art. Every year in June, Stone City has an art festival in his honor.

In spring and summer, bicycle racing is a fun sport. One big event is the RAGBRAI. This is a weeklong bike ride. During the RAGBRAI, thousands of people bike across the state.

During summer, Iowans also enjoy camping, fishing, and boating. In winter, some people like to ski and ice skate.

# GLOSSARY

**ancestors** — the people who lived in your family before you, such as your great-grandparents

**bluffs** — the high, steep banks of a river

**communities** — groups of people who live near each other

**effigy mounds** — burial mounds built in the shapes of animals

**erosion** — the process of wearing away soil and rock by wind or water

**glaciers** — large masses of ice that move slowly across land

**Great Depression** — a time during the 1930s when many people lost jobs and many businesses lost money

**habitats** — places where plants or animals live

**immigrants** — people who leave one country to live in another country

**industries** — types of businesses, such as selling insurance, farming, or making machinery

**lead** — a soft metal found in the ground

**legislature** — a group of people who make laws

**literacy** — the ability to read and write

**mine** — to dig minerals out of the ground

**prairies** — large areas of flat or rolling grassland with few or no trees

**territory** — area of land that belongs to a country

# TO FIND OUT MORE

## Books

*Critters of Iowa Pocket Guide.* Ann E. McCarthy (Adventure Publications)

*H is for Hawkeye: An Iowa Alphabet.* Discover America State by State (series). Patricia Pierce (Sleeping Bear Press)

*Iowa.* This Land Is Your Land (series). Ann Heinrichs (Compass Point Books)

*Iowa Facts and Symbols.* The States and Their Symbols (series). Elaine A. Kule (Bridgestone Books)

*Herbert Hoover.* Profiles of the Presidents (series). Michael Teitelbaum (Compass Point Books)

*The Mississippi River.* Rookie Read-About Geography (series). Allan Fowler (Children's Press)

## Web Sites

Enchanted Learning: Iowa
www.enchantedlearning.com/usa/states/iowa/

Iowa Department of Natural Resources: Kids' Pages
www.iowadnr.com/kids/index.html

Living History Farms
www.lhf.org/farmsites.html

U.S. Presidents: Herbert Hoover
www.whitehouse.gov/kids/presidents/herberthoover.html

# INDEX